CHOPIN-SCHAUM

BASED ON EVENTS AND EPISODES OF CHOPIN'S LIFE

The Purpose of the Chopin-Schaum Edition

Frédéric Chopin (1810–1849) composed his great music under abstract titles such as Preludes, Mazurkas, Berceuses, Waltzes, or another term that refers to the form of the piece. Modern education advocates graphic descriptive captions that tell incidents: that is why Mr. Schaum has substituted historically interesting titles for the abstract terms. The original titles are also included for every piece. This wealth of true biographical information adds musical appreciation to these authentic Chopin excerpts.

Teachers will be happy to note that this Chopin-Schaum book contains one or more examples of each musical form for which Chopin was famous.

Editor: Gail Lew
Production Coordinator: Karl Bork
Cover Illustration: Magdi Rodríguez
Cover Design: María A. Chenique

Contents

Index of Biographical Titles

Cradle Song (Berceuse, Op. 57) ..... RomAntic #7 3

Three Sisters (Prelude, Op. 28, No. 7) 4

Wonder Child of Warsaw (Rondo, Op. 1) 5

A Birthday Present (Mazurka, Op. 67, No. 3) 6

Skaters on the Ice-Bound Vistula
(Waltz, Op. 34, No. 3) 7

Little Dog Chasing His Tail
("Minute Waltz," Op. 64, No. 1) ..... CHOPIN #11 8

In an Old Polish Inn (Scherzo, Op. 31) 10

Farewell to Poland (Waltz, Op. 34, No. 2) 11

The Silver Urn (Theme from Concerto, Op. 11) ..... Romantic #9 12

Christmas in Paris (Mazurka, Op. 7, No. 1) 13

Hats Off, Gentlemen, a Genius
(Waltz, Op. 64, No. 2) 14

The Ballade of Lithuania
(Ballade, Op. 23) 16

English Concert Tour
("Military Polonaise," Op. 40, No. 1) 18

In Chopin's Studio (Impromptu, Op. 36) 20

Revolutionary Etude (Op. 10, No. 12) ..... CHOPIN #10 21

Island of Majorca
("Raindrop Prelude," Op. 28, No. 15) ..... Romantic #2 #3 CHOPIN 22

Summer at Nohant (Nocturne, Op. 15, No. 2) ..... Chopin #4 24

Warsaw Prelude (Op. 28, No. 20) 25

The Tragic Sonata (Op. 35) ..... CHOPIN #12 26

The King's Entrance March
(Polonaise, Op. 53) 30

Index of Musical Forms

Ballade (Op. 23) 18

Berceuse (Op. 57) 3

Concerto (Op. 11) 12

Etude
("Revolutionary Etude," Op. 10, No. 12) 21

Impromptu (Op. 36) 22

Mazurka (Op. 7, No. 1) 13

Mazurka (Op. 67, No. 3) 6

Nocturne (Op. 15, No. 2) 24

Polonaise
("Military Polonaise," Op. 40, No. 1) 18

Polonaise (Op. 53) 30

Prelude (Op. 28, No. 7) 4

Prelude ("Raindrop," Op. 28, No. 15) 22

Prelude (Op. 28, No. 20) 25

Rondo (Op. 1) 5

Scherzo (Op. 31) 10

Sonata (Op. 35) 26

Waltz (Op. 34, No. 2) 11

Waltz (Op. 34, No. 3) 7

Waltz
("Minute Waltz," Op. 64, No. 1) 8

Waltz (Op. 64, No. 2) 14

CRADLE SONG

Berceuse, Op. 57*

When you sing "The Star Spangled Banner" on February 22, in honor of George Washington, think of another great man who claims the same birthday — Frédéric Chopin (pronounced Show-Pan). Chopin was born in Poland in 1810, seventy eight years later than George Washington. That's a longtime ago, but the world is still playing his music today. This cradle song was called "Berceuse" by Chopin. A Berceuse is another name for cradle song or lullaby.

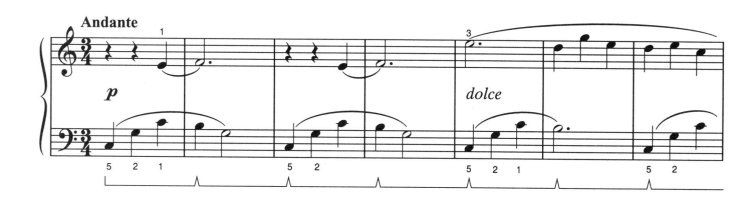

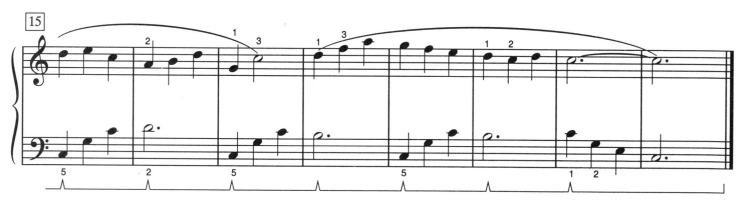

* The abbreviation Op. stands for Opus, meaning work. It is used in connection with numbers. Thus Op. 57 means Chopin's 57th work.

THREE SISTERS

Prelude, Op. 28, No. 7

Three sisters, Louise, Isabelle, and Emilia, with Frédéric made a busy household for Mother Chopin. The huge fireplace needed to be cleaned, and tallow candles made for light. The three sisters took turns at the spinning wheel. Frédéric began studying piano at the age of six, and you can be sure that he always practiced when came around.

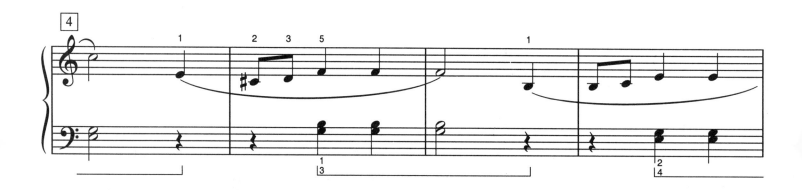

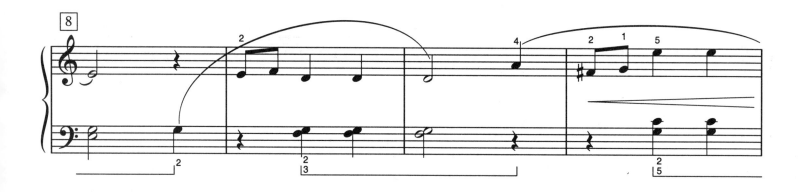

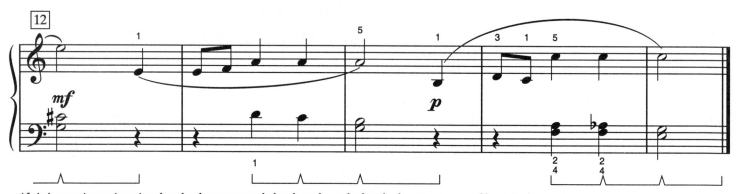

It is interesting to imagine that the three repeated chords at the end of each phrase represent Chopin's three sisters.

EL00277A

WONDER CHILD OF WARSAW

Rondo, Op. 1 - First published composition

The village people gave a concert to raise money for the poor. On the program was an eight year old boy–Frédéric Chopin. There he shyly sat in his new velvet suit with the lace trimmed collar and played "as easily as the birds sing." How surprised everyone was! Every lady wanted to kiss him! "The Wonder Child" and "Little Mozart" were his new nicknames.

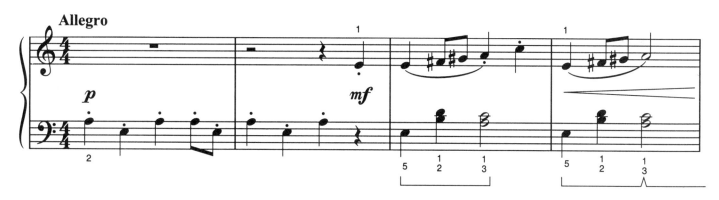

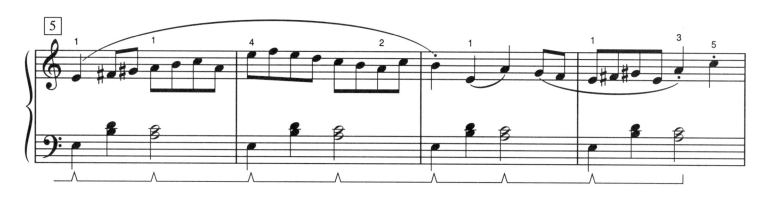

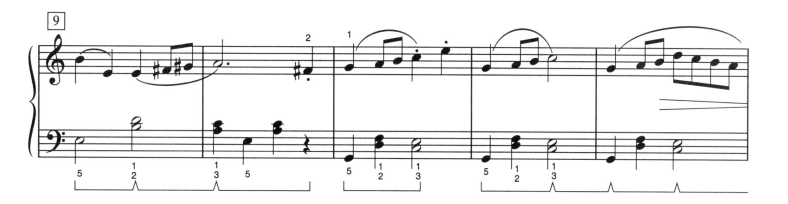

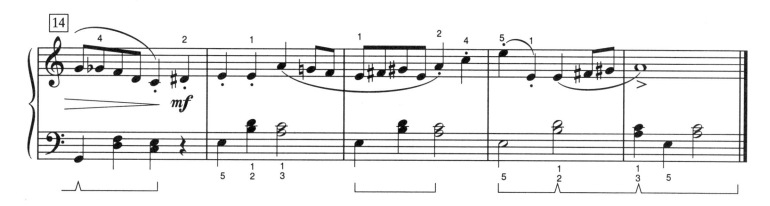

A BIRTHDAY PRESENT

Mazurka, Op. 67, No. 3

"Frédéric, how would you like to hear the greatest singer in Europe?" "Oh Daddy, really? Is Madame Catalani from Italy here?" Frédéric sat entranced at the golden voice beauty. He scarcely breathed, but when it was all over, and Catalani asked Frédéric to play for her, his bubble of happiness almost burst. As a remembrance on his birthday the great lady presented Chopin with a gold watch inscribed "Given by Madame Catalani to Frédéric Chopin, aged ten years."

SKATERS ON THE ICE-BOUND VISTULA

Waltz, Op. 34, No. 3

Do you like to skate? Chopin did! In fact, he ran away from his home one clear winter day to join the happy crowd on the Vistula River. The singing, the rhythm, the color all enthralled him so long that dinner was forgotten. Sister Louise suddenly brought him away from the icy fairyland and back to hot soup and the piano.

THE LITTLE DOG CHASING HIS TAIL

Waltz, Op. 64, No. 1 - Sometimes called Minute Waltz

Chopin's puppy cuddled quietly at Frédéric's feet during practice time, waiting for the jolly romp that always followed. Such wild scamperings! Such silly circlings trying to catch his tail! This was the happy memory that helped Chopin write the waltz "Little Dog Chasing His Tail."

9

IN AN OLD POLISH INN

Scherzo, Op. 31

Time lagged for Frédéric while new horses from a Polish Inn were made ready to draw the public coach. Then he found a piano! Suddenly the fellow travelers, the inn-keeper, and all the hired help were curiously silent. Who was this young man who played the Polish airs they loved in this new and intriguing manner? The horses were ready. The coach needed to continue, but the inn-keeper begged, "Please stay and give us your music! I, myself, will furnish you with a coach and horses to continue later." So Chopin stayed.

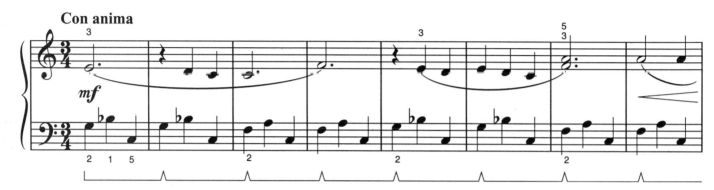

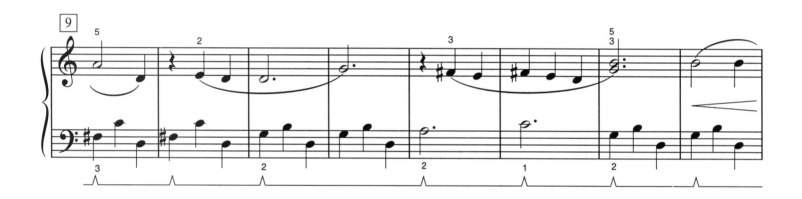

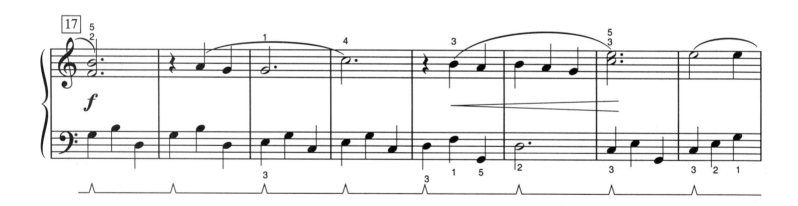

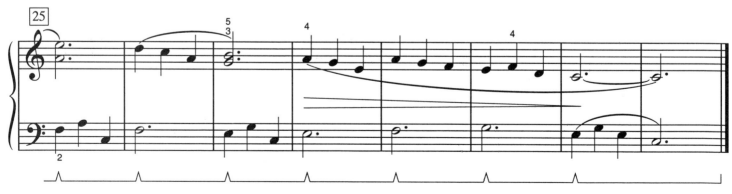

FAREWELL TO POLAND

Waltz, Op. 34, No. 2

Soon after Chopin was seventeen years old, he talked and dreamed of going to Paris. Leaving home, friends, and one special girl was harder than he realized. Each planned trip was cancelled until finally, when he was twenty, the farewell concert was announced. So many friends wanted to hear Chopin that three programs were needed to accomodate all the well-wishers. Chopin never returned to Poland.

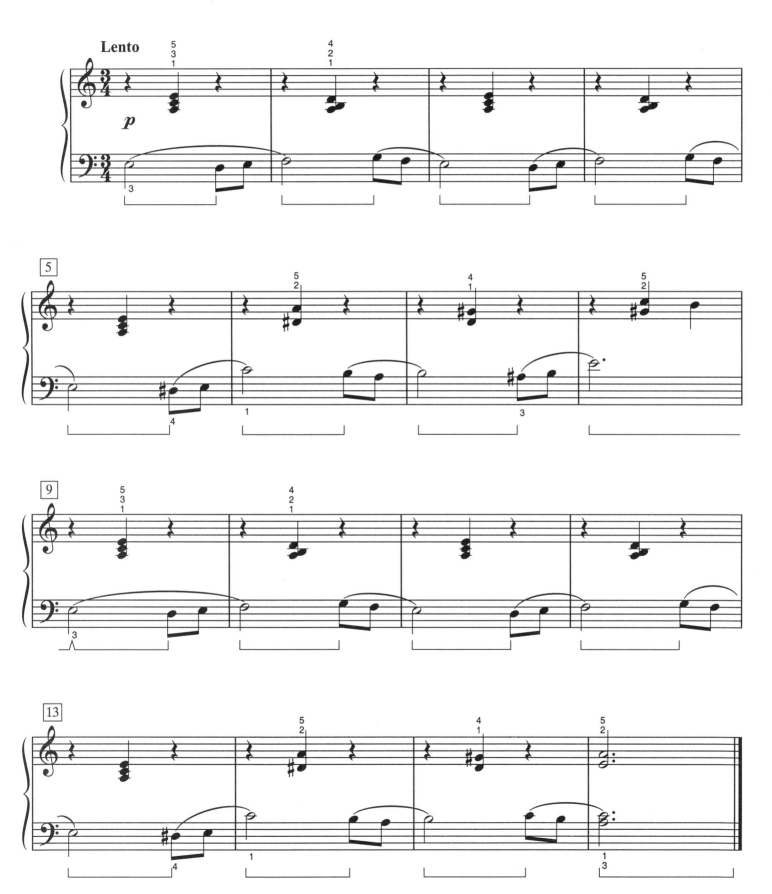

THE SILVER URN

Concerto, Op. 11

Chopin's neighbors loved him, especially because he took their Polish melodies and improvised* them into patriotic and exciting compositions. His music made them glad that they were Polish, and when he left them, they wanted him to remember his country. A beautiful silver urn, filled with Polish soil, was given to Chopin at his farewell concert. It always remained a keepsake to Frédéric.

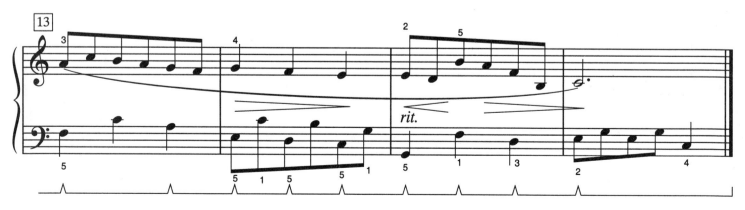

*im-pro-vized means to add and decorate by ear.

EL00277A

CHRISTMAS IN PARIS

Mazurka, Op. 7, No. 1

To thousands of people "Christmas In Paris" means gayety, excitement, and happy gatherings. To Frédéric, it meant a miserable day in bed treating a bad cough. Doctors didn't have the knowledge to help him, and he gradually became weaker and weaker until he finally contacted tuberculosis.

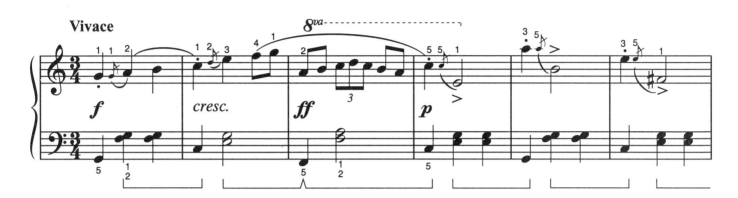

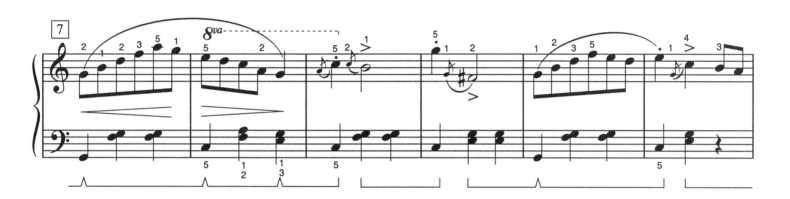

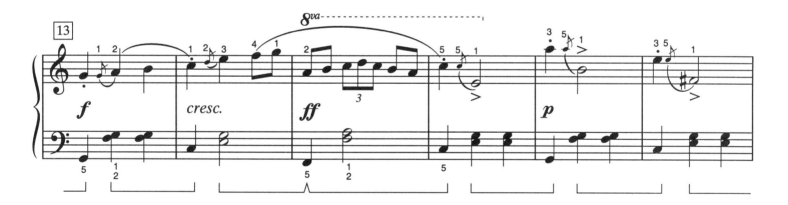

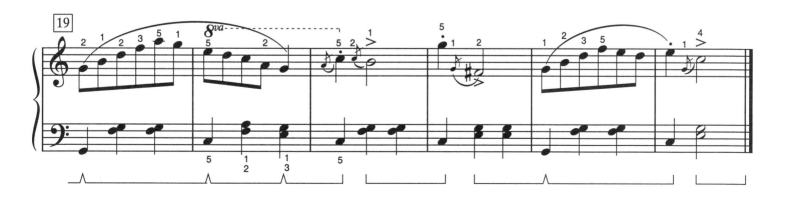

HATS OFF, GENTLEMEN, A GENIUS

Waltz, Op. 64, No. 2

It is generally easy for one to write or draw something that parents and friends admire. To write or draw something that real critics and artists approve is much harder. When Schumann, another famed composer, praised a Chopin waltz with, "Hats off, gentlemen, a genius," that judgement was worth much more to Chopin than even his mother's loving comments.

THE BALLADE OF LITHUANIA

Ballade, Op. 23

The word *ballade* can mean two different things. It may denote a poem that tells a story, or if this story is told in music instead of words, it also, is called ballade. This musical ballade tells of the worry and torment in the soul of Konrad of Lithuania. Konrad leaves the glory of a royal court to fight against it by joining the oppressed people of his own family and country. Chopin was the first composer who wrote in ballade form by creating mood pictures.

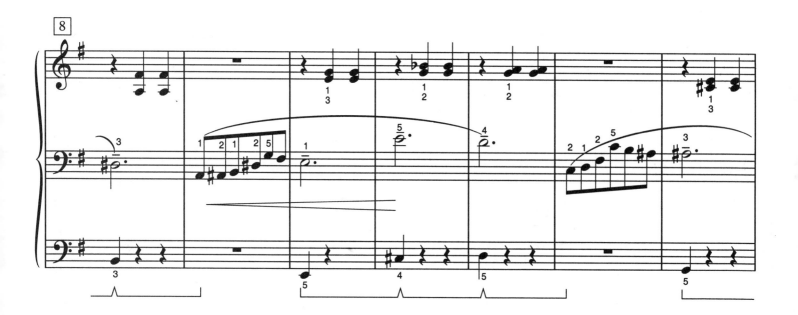

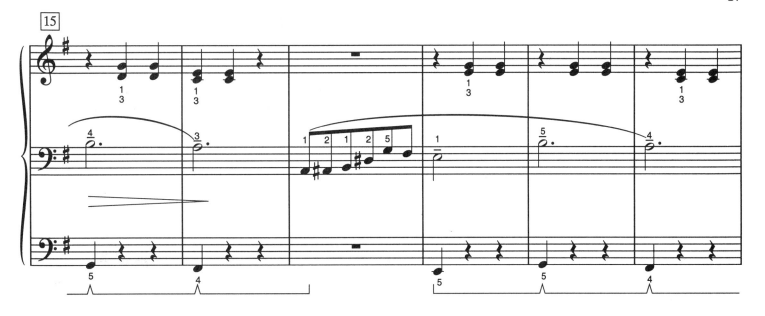

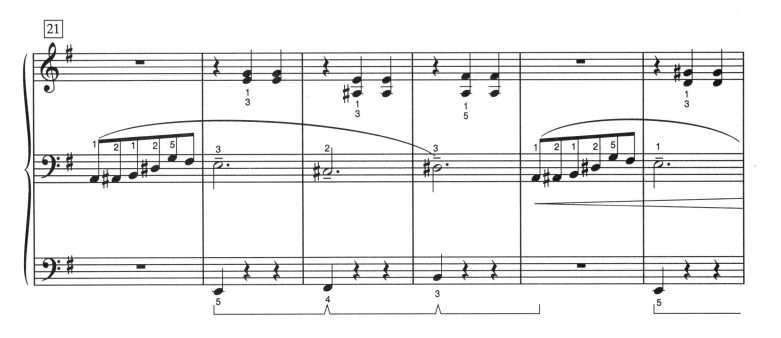

ENGLISH CONCERT TOUR

Military Polonaise, Op. 40, No. 1

Chopin was now a grown man, and his musical fame had stretched beyond Poland, Germany, and France. England welcomed him at private concerts and parties where society delighted in his elegant manners. Chopin rarely played in large concert halls; his light piano touch sounded best in the smaller rooms.

Allegro con brio

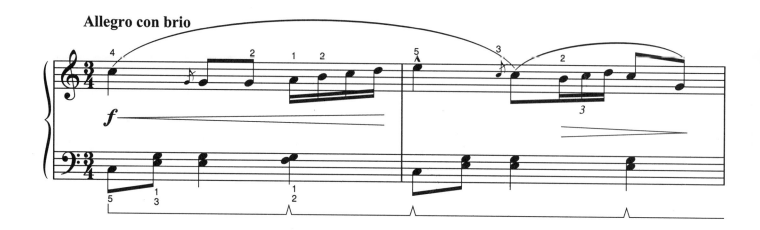

IN CHOPIN'S STUDIO

Impromptu, Op. 36

Chopin endured no cold attic room for his studio in Paris. He loved wealth and the fellowship of grand ladies and polite gentlemen. Chopin, personally, chose the pearl-grey paper for the walls, and lovingly fingered the velvet drapery at the windows. Pupils, mainly wealthy ladies, gathered daily for lessons, and polite society stopped at the Chopin studio to chat and drink tea.

REVOLUTIONARY ETUDE

Op. 10, No. 12

Filled with grief and worry over the Chopin family in Poland, Frédéric poured all his sorrow into this Revolutionary Etude when he heard that the enemy army had taken the Polish town where his parents and sisters lived.

THE ISLAND OF MAJORCA

Raindrop Prelude, Op. 28, No. 15

A wonderful vacation was planned for Chopin on the Island of Majorca. The sun would cure his cough, and Frédéric would have quiet days to compose. But, everything went wrong; the rented house was cold, food was poor, the piano was hopelessly out of tune, and it rained, and rained, and rained. Chopin wrote four preludes. This one suggests the constant dripping of the rain.

SUMMER AT NOHANT

Nocturne, Op. 15, No. 2

The dismal vacation at Majorca was forgotten after many pleasant rests at Nohant where Chopin was the guest of George Sand (Pen name of Madame Dudevant, a French woman novelist). Nohant was in the quiet country, and although Chopin loved the gayety of Paris, he wrote and accomplished much more in peaceful Nohant.

Could it be Magic Prelude

THE WARSAW PRELUDE

Op. 28, No. 20

There may be many reasons why Chopin wrote this grief stricken prelude. George Sand, a woman he loved, had left him, his father had died, and Chopin wasn't strong enough to travel back to Poland. Sick in heart and in mind, this composition was the result of his longings for home and loved ones.

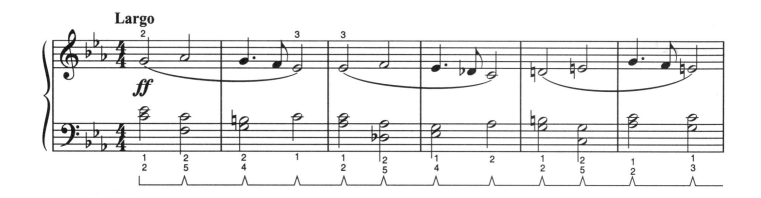

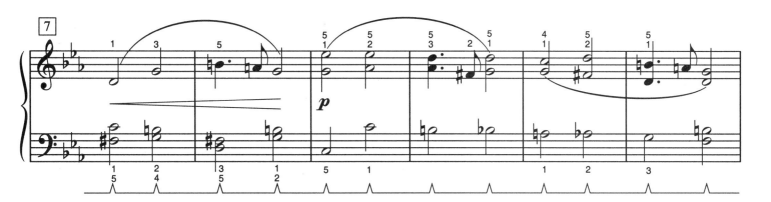

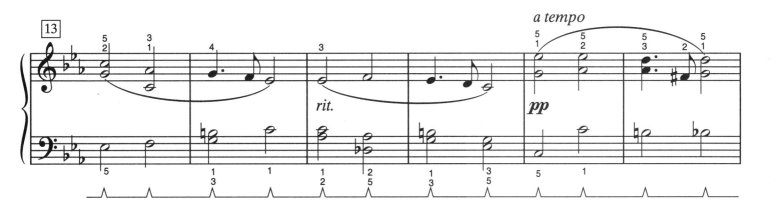

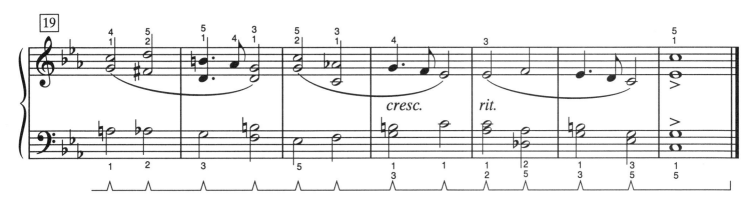

EL00277A

THE TRAGIC SONATA
Op. 35

The term *sonata* denotes a musical composition for solo instrument consisting of three or four independent pieces called *movements*. The movements are related by a general theme or mood. The striking mood of the "Tragic Sonata" is one of fear and disaster. Chopin died of tuberculosis when he was thirty-nine years old.

I. First Movement *(Fear of Death)*

II. Second Movement *(Triumph of Death)*

III. Third Movement *(Funeral March)*
Marche funébre

IV. Fourth Movement *(Wind Over the Graves)*

THE KING'S ENTRANCE MARCH

Polonaise, Op. 53

Chopin is known for not only his beautiful melodies, but also big and powerful pieces, such as this one that is befitting the music a monarch might hear when in a parade or entering a building. You can almost hear trumpet calls in the right hand, and the timpani in the left; all with an emphasis on beat one.

John W. Schaum
(1905–1988)

Founder and director of the Schaum Music School in Milwaukee, Wisconsin, John W. Schaum is the composer of internationally famous piano teaching materials including more than 200 books and 450 sheet music pieces. He is author of the internationally acclaimed *Schaum Piano Course* published by Belwin-Mills Publishing Corporation/ Warner Bros. Publications. During his extensive travels, Mr. Schaum has presented hundreds of piano teacher workshops in all fifty states. He was president of the Wisconsin Music Teachers Association and soloist with the Milwaukee Philharmonic Orchestra.

Mr. Schaum received a master of music degree from Northwestern University, a bachelor of music degree from Marquette University, and a bachelor of music education degree from the University of Wisconsin-Milwaukee.

He remains an important influence in the lives of hundreds of thousands of piano students who have enjoyed and continue to play his music.